PICTURE LIBRARY
HELICOPTERS

PICTURE LIBRARY
HELICOPTERS

N. S. Barrett

Franklin Watts

London   New York   Sydney   Toronto

CB
C602008699
J629.13.

© 1984 Franklin Watts Ltd

First published in Great Britain
    1984 by
Franklin Watts Ltd
12a Golden Square
London W1

First published in the USA by
Franklin Watts Inc
387 Park Avenue South
New York
N.Y. 10016

First published in Australia by
Franklin Watts
1 Campbell Street
Artarmon, NSW 2064

UK ISBN: 0 86313 133 6
US ISBN: 0-531-03721-5
Library of Congress Catalog Card
    Number: 84-50698

Printed in Italy

Designed by
McNab Design

Photographs by
Aérospatiale
B.P. Oil Ltd
Bell Helicopter Textron
Boeing Vertol Company
Bristow Helicopters Ltd
J. M. G. Gradidge
Novosti Press Agency
Westland Helicopters

Illustrated by
Tony Bryan

Technical Consultant
J. M. G. Gradidge

Contents

Introduction

Helicopters are flying machines with moving wings. The wings are called "rotors", because they go around in a circle. Rotors allow a helicopter to take off straight from the ground into the air. An ordinary aeroplane, with "fixed wings", cannot do this. It has to gain speed along the ground. It can take off only when it is going fast enough.

△ A helicopter hovers over troops during an army exercise. Helicopters have many uses in both war and peace.

Helicopters can do many other things that ordinary aeroplanes cannot do. They can land on small spaces and on rough ground. Helicopters can fly backwards or sideways. They can "hover" in one spot in the air. Because of this, they have many special uses.

△ A helicopter flies over a busy city on its way to the airport. It is the same model as the military one on the opposite page, a Westland 30.

The helicopter

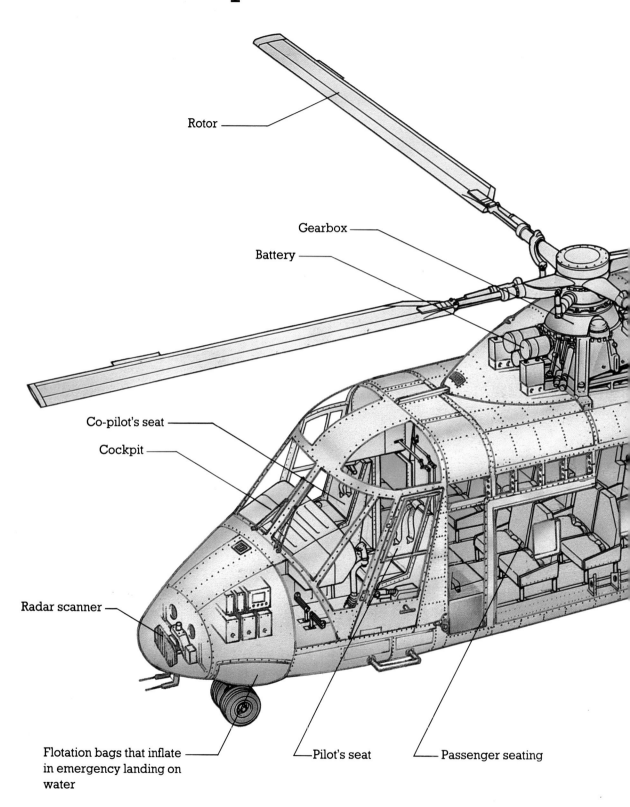

Rotor

Gearbox

Battery

Co-pilot's seat

Cockpit

Radar scanner

Flotation bags that inflate
in emergency landing on
water

Pilot's seat

Passenger seating

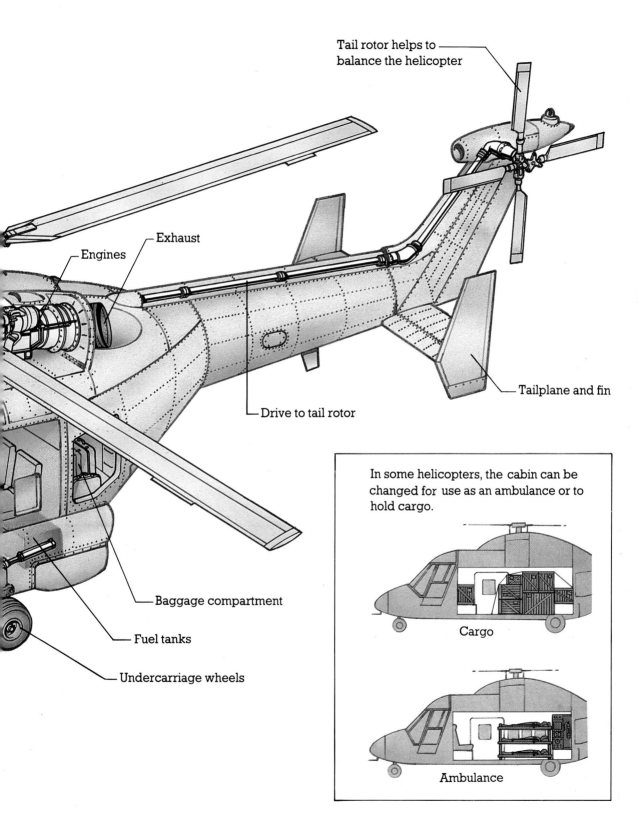

Tail rotor helps to
balance the helicopter

Exhaust

Engines

Tailplane and fin

Drive to tail rotor

Baggage compartment

Fuel tanks

Undercarriage wheels

In some helicopters, the cabin can be
changed for use as an ambulance or to
hold cargo.

Cargo

Ambulance

Types of helicopter

Most helicopters have one rotor in front and a smaller rotor on the tail. Some big helicopters have two large rotors, one at the front and one at the back. Another type has two rotors at the front. They are on each side of the body, like the wings of a plane. Helicopters are built in many different sizes, depending on what they are going to be used for.

▷ A helicopter prepares to land on the "helipad" of an oil rig. Helicopters are used for carrying workers and supplies to oil rigs.

▽ An AS 355 Twinstar helicopter has a main rotor at the front and a small rotor on its tail. It has "skids" underneath to stop it rolling when landing on uneven ground.

▷ The Boeing Vertol 234 is one of the largest passenger-carrying helicopters, with room for 44 people. It has main rotors at back and front called tandem rotors. These craft are called Chinooks when used for warfare.

Some flying machines with rotors are not true helicopters. These include "convertiplanes" and "autogyros". The convertiplane can fly as a helicopter or an aeroplane. It has two rotors, fitted on fixed wings. The rotors can be tilted forward to act as propellers. This changes the craft from a helicopter into an aeroplane, which can travel much faster.

△ The Bell 301 is a test aircraft. It has rotors that can be tilted. Here it is flying as a helicopter. The pilot can turn the craft into an aeroplane when it has reached a safe height and is moving fast enough. This is done by gradually turning the rotors forward. Such craft are called "convertiplanes".

"Autogyros" are small craft with a rotor on top and a propeller in front. The engine drives the propeller, not the rotor as in true helicopters. The rotor turns round by itself. The pilot starts it by hand or with the engine. An autogyro takes off by moving along the ground, just like a plane. But the rotor lifts it upward to help it take off more quickly.

△ Autogyros are flown for fun. They are mostly flown by one person. Here, Wing Commander K. H. Wallis flies his own design, the WA-116. Wallis has designed and built a whole series of autogyros.

Passenger helicopters

Lightweight helicopters carry as few as two people, including the pilot. Most helicopters carry 10–30 people. The biggest passenger craft can carry about 50 passengers. They are known as "heavy-lift" helicopters. Some troop-carrying helicopters can ferry more than 100 men.

▽ Helicopters take people to work on an oil rig at sea. Offshore oil rigs have a special landing pad for helicopters. It is usually safer and faster to travel by air than by boat in rough seas.

Helicopters built to carry passengers have many uses. Because they can land in small spaces, they can be used in city centres. "Heliports" are sometimes built on top of buildings. People fly between these helicopter stations and airports. Small offshore islands may also be reached by helicopter. Business people often use helicopters for short trips.

△ The flight-deck of a Sikorsky S-76, showing the pilot's and co-pilot's seats and the instrument panel. The instruments are like those in a plane. But a helicopter is harder to fly, because it can hover and move in all directions.

Helicopters are often used for pleasure trips. They can hover above a spot to give passengers time to enjoy the scenery. They can also land easily at places of special interest, often in areas that cannot be reached by cars.

△ Helicopters are often the fastest means of transport between big cities. This Bell 222 is flying over Dallas, in the USA.

△Helicopters may be
used for sightseeing.
They can take people
close to beautiful
scenery.

◁The cabin of a
passenger helicopter
usually has plenty of
room. Seats may be
removed for carrying
cargo.

Working helicopters

Helicopters are used for many different tasks. Police use them to check on traffic or to spot offences on the roads, such as speeding. They can be used for herding cattle on big ranches. Other uses include taking supplies to lighthouses and spraying water on forest fires.

▽Helicopters are used for spraying crops with chemicals. Farmers use these chemicals to kill pests or to help crops grow.

Another important job for helicopters is lifting and carrying heavy loads. Goods and equipment may be carried inside or slung from a wire under the body. Special helicopters are used as cranes. They can lift heavy machinery and equipment such as bulldozers. Some can even lift sections of bridges or small houses.

△ A large helicopter such as this Bell 205A-1 can lift as much as 2 tonnes, the weight of two average cars. Special "crane" helicopters can lift 10 tonnes or more.

Combat helicopters

Helicopters were first used in battle to take injured men to hospital. This is still an important job for combat helicopters, but now they do other things as well. They move supplies, ammunition and troops. They are also used to spot enemy movements and weapons. Some helicopters are armed with guns or rockets. They can be used over land or sea.

▽ An AS 332B Super Puma lands troops in a clearing. This army version of the Puma carries 24 troops, and has room for stretchers. It may be armed with two 20 mm cannon or with rocket launchers.

△A Chinook with Spanish Army markings. Boeing has built hundreds of Chinooks for use all over the world. They hold more than 40 troops, and can carry heavy loads slung underneath the fuselage.

◁The navy form of the Super Puma (AS 332F) is used to attack warships. It may be armed with two missiles.

◁A Lynx helicopter of the British Royal Navy lands on a destroyer. The Lynx has many uses, including search-and-rescue work. It is also used to guard ships, and to attack enemy submarines and surface vessels.

To the rescue

Rescue helicopters save many lives every year. Their pilots sometimes risk their own lives to pick up people in trouble. They often rescue people from sinking ships. Rescue helicopters can reach climbers stranded on mountains or people cut off by forest fires. If helicopters cannot land, they drop a ladder or a rope.

△ The French Dauphin 2 is used by the US Coast Guard. Coast guard helicopters often go to the rescue of people in trouble at sea.

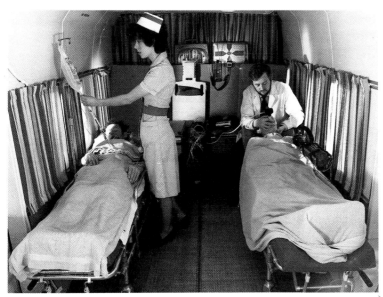

△ The Sea King is often used for search-and-rescue work. It can hover steadily in fierce winds and weather. A rescue hoist winds people up to safety.

◁ The Westland 30 may be rigged out as an air ambulance. After a rescue, medical staff in the cabin can treat injured survivors on the way to hospital.

The story of helicopters

The first helicopters

A Frenchman named Paul Cornu invented a machine with two rotors in 1907. He managed to lift it straight up off the ground to a height of about 2 m (6 ft). This was the first helicopter "flight". It took place four years after the first aeroplane flight.

Autogyros

Early helicopters did not work very well. The first successful craft to make use of a rotor were invented in Spain by Juan de la Cierva. He called them "Autogiros". They worked in the same way as the autogyros of today.

△ A Cierva "Autogiro" (C17) of more than 50 years ago.

Success

The first helicopters to take off and stay in the air for a reasonable length of time were built in the 1930s. The German inventor Henrich Focke built a machine with two main rotors. In 1937, he flew it for more than an hour.

Sikorsky

One of the first helicopter designers was a Russian called Igor Sikorsky. He moved to the USA and built aeroplanes. Then, in 1939, he designed the Sikorsky VS-300. This was a single-seater helicopter with a main rotor and a tail rotor. It was the first of the true helicopters as we know them today.

△ The Sikorsky S-62A made its first flight in 1958. The Sikorsky company was the first to make a profit from carrying passengers.

The Rotodyne

The Rotodyne was a cross between an aeroplane and a helicopter. This "convertiplane" was built by a British company called Fairey Aviation. Like a helicopter, it had a rotor to lift it off the ground. But like an aeroplane, it had two propellers

△The Rotodyne.

helicopter. As it gathers speed, the pilot tilts the rotors forward so that they act as propellers. It can fly at more than twice the speed of most true helicopters. The Model 301 is still being tested. It is hoped that convertiplanes with tilting rotors will have uses in peace as well as in combat.

for level flight. It was very much faster than ordinary helicopters. The Rotodyne project came to an end in 1962.

Tilting rotors

In the 1970s, the US Army built a new type of convertiplane. This is the Bell Model 301, also called the XV-15. It looks like a fixed-wing aeroplane with engines mounted on its wing tips. The engines drive rotors, so the craft can take off and hover like a

△A Bell helicopter with special landing gear. This consists of tubes that can be inflated with air like balloons if the helicopter has to land on water in an emergency.

△A Bell Model 301 with its rotors just starting to tilt forward.

△The CH-13 Labrador has tandem rotors.

Facts and records

△ The Aérospatiale SA 315B Lama is the world's highest flying helicopter.

Highest climb

A helicopter has climbed to a height of more than 12 km (7½ miles). This record was set by a French helicopter, the SA 315B Lama.

Fastest and largest

The world's fastest helicopter is the Russian Mil Mi-24. It has flown at 368 km/h (229 mph), about the speed of a fast sports car.

The Russians have also built the largest helicopters. The Mi-12 has rotors set side by side. The span across the tips of the rotors is 67 m (220 ft). This is about the same width as an average football pitch.

Payloads

A helicopter's "payload" is the weight it can carry. As helicopters have been improved, they have been able to carry greater payloads. About 40 years ago, they could just lift about 100 kg (220 lb), the weight of a big man. In 1982, a Mil Mi-26 lifted a record of 56 tonnes, equal to the weight of 10 big elephants.

Code names

Russian helicopters are usually built in secret. They are known in the western world by code names, all beginning with the letter "H". These names include Hare (Mil Mi-1), Hound (Mi-4), Hook (Mi-6), Hip (Mi-8), Homer (Mi-12) and Halo (Mi-26). The Mil series was started by the designer Mikhail Mil.

△ A Mil crane helicopter.

Glossary

Amphibian
A helicopter that can take off and land on water as well as land.

Autogyro
A flying machine that uses a propeller for power and a rotor to help it stay in the air. Autogyros cannot hover like a helicopter, because their rotors are turned by the air – like the arms of a windmill.

Convertiplane
A helicopter that may be converted into an aeroplane after take-off, and back into a helicopter for hovering or landing. This is usually done by having rotors that tilt.

Floats
An undercarriage for landing on water. Many helicopters have "flotation bags", which inflate in an emergency landing on water and act as floats.

Fuselage
The body of an aircraft.

Heliport
A special landing and take-off station for helicopters. A landing area without fuel pumps or workshops is called a "helipad".

Hover
To hang in the air without moving in any direction. Helicopters can hover, aeroplanes cannot.

Lift
The force that raises an aircraft off the ground and keeps it in the air. In helicopters, the lift is provided by rotors.

Rotor
Rotors are the spinning wings of a helicopter or autogyro. In helicopters, rotors are driven by the engine. A rotor has 2 to 8 blades.

Skids
Undercarriage gear that looks like tubes. It is used for landing on rough ground.

Tandem rotors
A helicopter with rotors "in tandem" has two main rotors, one at the front and one at the back, like riders on a tandem bicycle.

Tilt rotor
A rotor that can be tilted to act as a propeller in flight.

Index